UNDERSTANDING THE TIMES

STUDENT WORKBOOK

Authors
Mike Sligh • Paul Pyle

Managing Editor
Sharon R. Berry, Ph.D.

Based on the work of Dr. David A. Noebel, *Understanding the Times:
The Religious Worldviews of Our Day and the Search for Truth*

TABLE OF CONTENTS

INTRODUCTION TO WORLDVIEWS

The Battle for Hearts and Minds

Read Chapter 1 and answer the following questions.

1. List two ways Christianity is different from other worldviews.

    a. _____

    _____

    _____

    b. _____

    _____

    _____

2. Which two worldviews are atheistic?

    a. _____

    b. _____

3. Which worldview is described as the ultimate religion of self?

    _____

Bible Study: What the Bible Says About the Existence of God

1. The word translated fool in Psalms denotes one who is morally inferior, that is, one who cannot or will not make accurate distinctions between right and wrong. According to Psalm 14:1, what secret thought about God does the **fool** harbor in his heart? Why would atheism be attractive to someone who is "morally inferior"?

   _____

   _____

   _____

   _____

2. We often judge an artist by the work he or she produces. According to Psalm 19:1–3, the skies "declare . . . proclaim . . . display" many facts concerning God and His glory. In your opinion, what does the universe say about God? According to the Psalmist, which cultures have access to nature's magnificent testimony to the glory of God (v. 4)?

   _____

   _____

   _____

   _____

3. According to Romans 1, which of the following does the Apostle Paul consider Exhibit A in the question of the existence of God?

   - *wide-spread belief in God*
   - *the existence of the universe*
   - *man's moral sense (conscience)*

What did men do with their knowledge of God? What does Paul mean when he says that men are "without excuse"? What effect did denying God have on their thinking (v. 21)?

_____

_____

_____

4. According to Romans 1:18, what provokes the wrath of God?

_____

5. Romans 1:20 lists two of God's "eternal qualities" revealed in nature. What are they? What are some important attributes of God *not* revealed in nature?

_____

_____

Lecture Notes: Introduction to Secular Humanism

I. Definition: the view that since God _____ it is up to

mankind alone to _____.

II. History of Humanism

A. _____

1. "You will be _____ ."

2. Part of ancient _____, _____, and _____philosophies.

B. _____: The _____

1. *Humanist Manifesto* in 1933

a. Rejection of _____.

b. Great optimism that mankind could achieve _____

_____ apart from _____.

c. Endorsed by small group of _____.

2. *Humanist Manifesto II* in 1973

a. _____ between 1933 and 1973 which called into

question _____ of first *Manifesto* and made it

necessary to write second manifesto.

b. _____: addressed more _____

_____, issues.

c. _____: endorsed by dozens of people, including

many_____.

C. _____: the secular humanist's agenda to _____.

1. Expanded _____.

a. Right to _____and _____.

b. Right to _____, _____, and _____.

2. _____(socialist economy).

3. _____.

Read Chapter 3 and answer the following questions:

1. Why did Isaac Asimov hesitate for so long to admit that he is an atheist? Why did he finally decide to admit his atheism?

    _____

    _____

2. How has the atheism of John Dewey so profoundly influenced American culture?

    _____

    _____

3. If a small child brought you a copy of Brockman's book, how would *you* explain the difference between believing in God and believing in dragons and fairies?

    _____

    _____

4. What is the difference between "believing in God" and "believing there is a God"?

    _____

    _____

5. We discussed positive and negative implications of atheism (the theological foundation of secular humanism). According to the text, what is "the necessary theological conclusion" to which theology must lead?

    _____

    _____

Bible Study: Christian Theology and Workplace Relationships

We have seen how Marxists interpret employer-employee relationships in an atheistic context. How does a Christian theistic worldview play out in such relationships? From the texts listed below, develop a list of essential principles that apply to the question of how Christian employees ought to treat their "masters" (employers) and how Christian employers, supervisors and managers ought to treat their subordinates. Create one list of rules for employees and another for employers.

> 1 Peter 2:18–21
> Ephesians 6:5–8
> Colossians 3:22–25
> 1 Timothy 6:1–2
> Titus 2:9–10

Be prepared to share the results of your study with the class.

Enrichment Activity: Letter from College

Your son is a nineteen-year-old student at a state university. He has written you the letter shown below. How would you answer him?

Dear Dad,

My first month of classes has been busy, but things have settled down a little now. I'm beginning to get the hang of dorm life, I think, and I'm beginning to enjoy my classes.

But there's one class that bothers me a little, actually one teacher. Dr. Forbes is probably the brightest and certainly the most popular instructor on campus. He's young, he's entertaining and he's very intelligent.

The other day in class he made an off-hand comment about what he called "the God concept." He didn't exactly attack Christianity; he just made it sound as if believing in God is something for insecure, backward people who need to believe in something.

I've never really thought about why I believe in God. I'd hate to think my whole religious experience is just a "psychological need fulfillment," as Dr. Forbes calls it.

This sort of thing comes up in the dorm when we're just sitting around talking about stuff late at night. Sometimes I think the only reason I believe anything is because you guys did such a good job at home teaching me what to believe.

It's getting late. I've got to hit the sack; test in Forbes' class tomorrow.

Love,

John

Bible Study: How Man Has Responded to God's Revelation

From the moment man rebelled against God, there have been communication problems between God and man. From the passages of Scripture listed below, match the negative ways people have responded to God's attempts to communicate.

Genesis 3:8–10	persecuting the prophet
Genesis 37:5–11	
Exodus 3–4	hesitating, questioning, negotiating
Deuteronomy 18:16	
Judges 6	outright disobedience
Jonah 1:1–3	
Jeremiah 38:1–6	fear
Matthew 14:3–5	
	ridicule

Read Chapter 6 and answer the following questions.

1. What are the two foundations on which Christian theism rests?

2. What are some of the differences between general and special revelation?

3. What does it mean that general revelation is "a necessary but insufficient means for providing knowledge about the Creator and His character"?

4. What sorts of evidence for the inspiration of Scripture are listed in the text?

5. What sorts of questions cannot be answered by general revelation but must be answered by special revelation?

6. What is "God's most direct form of special revelation"?

7. What is a "linchpin"? How is special revelation "the linchpin of Christianity"? How does general revelation function as a "prod"?

8. What did C. S. Lewis mean when he said, "Unless I believe in God, I can't believe in thought"?

Bible Study: Inspiration of Scripture

1. From 2 Timothy 3:14–17, what are some of the things the Scripture can do in the life of the believer? (List at least five specific answers from the passage.)

    _____

    _____

    _____

2. The clearest Biblical description of how the inspiration of the Scripture took place can be found in 2 Peter 1:21. Peter uses both negative and positive descriptions to explain the process. What is the negative description? What is the positive description?

    _____

    _____

    _____

3. In 2 Peter 1:21, the word translated **moved** (NIV **carried along**) is the same one used in Acts 27:15 to describe a physical process. What is that physical process? How does it illustrate the spiritual process by which the Scriptures were produced?

    _____

    _____

    _____

4. The first three verses of Hebrews 1 contrast the revelation given through the prophets with the revelation given through Christ. The Greek phrase translated "at various times and in different ways" emphasizes the piece-meal and fragmentary nature of the revelation given through the prophets. How is the revelation given through Christ (the Son) different?

    _____

    _____

    _____

Attributes of God

Using the information given in the text, give the term for each of the following descriptions of God's attributes.

1. sorrowful, angry, compassionate, jealous, able to show satisfaction

2. evidenced by God's works in creation and providence

3. three co-existent, co-eternal persons in one, equal in purpose and essence

4. sovereign in regard to His will

5. willingness to delay judgment

6. keeping promises

7. distinguishing between good and evil

Many people have fuzzy, inaccurate notions about who God is and what He is like; the statements below express some of those notions. For each statement, identify an attribute and passage of Scripture (from the text) which refutes the inaccurate idea about God. (The first one is done for you.)

1. God is just waiting for me to mess up so that He can zap me!
   When it's time for judgment, God has longsuffering patience. Exodus 32:11–14, John 10:28.

2. God just wants everyone to get along; He's not so uptight about sin.

3. God could never forgive me for what I've done.

4. I'm not sure I can rely on God.

5. You can't do anything to upset God. He's God!

Scripture Review

Give the Bible reference (book and chapter) for each sentence.

1. The fool says in his heart, "There is no God."

2. Scripture is useful for doctrine.

3. Holy men of God wrote as they were "carried along" by the Holy Spirit.

4. The heavens declare the glory of God.

5. There is no culture where the heavens have not declared the glory of God.

6. All Scripture is "God-breathed."

7. The existence of the universe is sufficient evidence for the existence of God.

8. Scripture is useful for correction.

9. Wicked men suppressed the obvious truth about God manifested in nature.

Terminology Review

Match phrase to term.
1. nature
2. denial that God exists
3. belief in God
4. limited accessibility
5. belief that all is God
6. example: Scripture
7. Marxist Theology
8. New Age Theology
9. specific content
10. declares God's glory
11. ultimate expression: Christ
12. belief that I am God

a. pantheism

b. theism

c. atheism

d. general revelation

e. special revelation

Lecture Notes: Recognizing Philosophical Assumptions

I. Definition: Assumption: _____   _____

   _____

II. Description: Assumptions

   A. Generally cannot be _____ or _____,
       but must be taken as articles of faith.

   B. Serve as basis for further _____ and _____.

   C. Are of two types:

      1. _____: One is _____ that one
          believes in the assumption and could _____
          (but not prove) why he does.

      2. _____: One believes _____
          _____
       and could not explain why he believes it.

Enrichment Activity: The Boys in the Box

Once there was a group of seven boys who had grown up in a rather large Box. Neither they nor anyone they knew had ever been Outside The Box and returned to tell about it.

One day one of the boys became curious about the shape of his world, the large Box. He got out some tools — a ruler, a calculator, and some paper — and began to measure, calculate and sketch a drawing of The Box as well as he could figure it. When he finished, he knew he had something special and he wished to show it to someone else.

He found one of his friends right away and told him, "I've found it! I have measured, calculated and sketched an accurate rendering of the shape of The Box!"

His friend, looked at the sketch, scratched his chin contemplatively and said, "Hmmm. . . . ." Then his friend took out an old piece of paper, obviously worn and yellowed by years of storage and opened it. It, too, contained a drawing. "This paper," said Boy 2, "was given to me by my father, who said it had been in the family for countless generations. This is the drawing of The Box as my family has understood it for many centuries."

The two boys compared the two drawings. There were so many similarities that it was obvious the drawings were of the same thing, yet there were some significant differences. The two boys couldn't tell from looking at the two drawings which one was more accurate. They were in the midst of what philosophers would call an epistemological dilemma: two ways of knowing, two slightly different renderings. Which, if either of them, could be trusted ? So the two of them set out to solve their puzzle.

They went to Boy 3, explained their difficulty, showed him their two drawings, and asked him what he thought. "I don't know if I can help or not," he said, drawing a piece of paper from his pocket. "This is what I've always believed The Box looks like." He showed them another drawing of The Box. This one, too, was similar in many significant respects but different in some ways as well.

"Where did you get *your* picture?" asked Boys 1 and 2 simultaneously.

"I just thought about it for a long time," answered Boy 3, "and I realized that this is simply the only way it *could* be. This is the only drawing that makes sense." He carefully explained the reasoning behind every line in his picture, but he acknowledged that the first Boy's drawing, based on measurement and calculation, and the second Boy's drawing, accepted by countless generations as the true picture of The Box, could also be the right drawing. Now the three of them had an even more complicated epistemological dilemma. What could they do but set out to seek the Answer?

Soon the trio found Boy 4 and explained their problem. Boy 4 thought for a moment, drew forth from his pocket a blank sheet of paper and quickly sketched a drawing of The Box. "This," he announced, "is what The Box actually looks like."

"How do you *know?*" the other three demanded.

"I don't *know* how I know," confessed Boy 4. "I just know. Doesn't it just seem right to you?" The other boys compared the four drawings and admitted that the new addition seemed as good a picture as any of the other three, but they still had no idea which one of the pictures, if any, accurately portrayed The Box. So they set out to find the Answer.

When they found Boy 5, showed him their pictures and explained their problem, they were not the least surprised when he pulled a piece of paper from his pocket. "This," he announced with an air of finality, "is what you've been looking for." Sure enough, it was a very fine drawing of The Box, similar to the others they had collected, but the boys had their one crucial question.

"That's a very fine drawing of The Box," they told him. "Where did it come from?"

"What do you mean, 'Where did it come from?'" he asked haughtily. "Can't you see the signature? This drawing was produced by a man who has a 200 I.Q. and is an expert on almost everything, and if he says this is what The Box looks like, this is what The Box looks like!"

For Boy 5, that fact settled the issue, but the other boys weren't so sure. Their uncertainty finally shook Boy 5, who began to wonder how he could be so sure his picture was so much more accurate than the others. Now all five boys set out to find the Answer.

When they found Boy 6, he was no help at all. He thought they were all wasting their time. "No one knows what The Box looks like," he scoffed, "and no one will ever know because no one can ever know. You are dumb to even try!" He declined, of course, to continue with them on their quest.

When they found Boy 7, they explained their problem, but without much enthusiasm. Their search so far had only made their puzzle more complicated, and they didn't have much hope that this boy would be able to help.

When Boy 7 said, "I have a picture of The Box," no one was surprised. But when they asked him where he got his picture, he told them, "Someone Outside The Box sent it to me." This statement startled the boys, for they had never thought of seeking counsel from Someone Outside The Box, but they all acknowledged that they could never hope to find a better source of information about The Box than that. Boy 7 explained that the Maker of The Box had told him what The Box was like.

But Boy 7 had more startling news. "Not only do I know what The Box looks like," he said, "but I also can tell you what else is Out There." He went on to tell his dumbstruck friends about things like rivers, clouds, stars, and other things they had never seen Inside The Box.

Now they began to compare their pictures to the picture given from Outside The Box. They could see places where their renderings were inaccurate or slightly out of proportion, and some of them began to make corrections on their drawings, while others hesitated, not willing to admit that their drawing might need correction. This started a new Debate — this time about whether there really was a Maker of The Box and whether such a Maker would *want* to say anything to the Boys in The Box and whether they should correct their drawings according to the picture from Outside The Box.

And to this very day, that Debate continues. No one knows how it will end, except Boy 7, who says with a smile that he knows how the Debate will end, because Someone Outside The Box told him.

Questions: The Boys in The Box

1. In a fable like this one, story elements symbolize things. In this story, what do the following story elements symbolize:

   - The Box: _____

   - The communication from Outside The Box: _____

   - The drawings of The Box: _____

2. Match each of the Boys to one of these sources of knowledge:

   - Which Boy appealed to culture?   _____

   - Which Boy appealed to a witness?   _____

   - Which Boy appealed to experience?   _____

   - Which Boy appealed to reason?   _____

   - Which Boy appealed to intuition?   _____

   - Which Boy appealed to revelation?   _____

Lecture Notes: A Few Good Answers

Just as we have done with epistemology—we have identified the few answers which can be given to the question "How do we know?" —we can now do with the other basic worldview assumptions. When this lecture is finished, we will have assembled a sort of philosophical menu with a mixture of true, false and incomplete assumptions. As the course progresses, we will find that many of these ideas and terms are answers given by various worldviews.

I. Epistemology: Six ways of acquiring knowledge

    A. _____

    B. _____

    C. _____

    D. _____

    E. _____

    F. _____

II. Cosmology: Three accounts of the beginning of everything

    A. _____

    B. _____

    C. No _____ or _____

III. Ontology: Three answers to the question, "What is real?"

    A. All is _____

    B. All is _____

    C. Both _____ and _____ are real.

IV. Ethics: Six sources of moral values.

    A. _____

    B. _____

    C. _____("_____")

    D. _____

    E. _____

    F. _____

V. Theology:

    A. Three answers to the question, "Does God exist?"

        1. God _____ (_____)

        (_____)

        2. _____whether God exists.

        (_____) (_____)

        3. There is a God. (_____) (_____)

    B. Three answers to the question, "What is God like?"

        1. God is _____. (_____)

        2. God is _____ (_____) (_____)

        3. _____is God.(_____)

        (_____)

VI. Anthropology:

    A. Three answers to the question, "What is Man?"

        1. Man is _____only, no _____

        (_____)

        2. Man is _____; matter is_____

        (_____)

        3. Man is both _____ and _____

B. Three descriptions of man's moral nature.

   1. Man's moral nature is _____

    (_____)

   2. Man is _____. (_____)

   3. Man's moral nature is _____. (_____

VII. History

  A. Two answers to the question, "Where is history going?"

    1. History is _____and _____(with

     beginning, middle and _____.

     (_____, _____)

    2. History is _____ and _____(with

     no beginning or end, not moving toward a conclusion).

  B. Three answers to the question, "Why do things happen as they do?"

    1. History is controlled by _____. (_____)

    2. History is controlled by _____

     (_____, _____), (_____)

    3. History is controlled by _____

     ("_____") (_____)

VIII. Death: Three accounts of what happens to humans after death.

  A. _____ (_____)

  B. _____ (_____)

  C. _____ (_____)

Terminology Review

Match the question to the term. Some questions may involve more than one term. Since these areas of philosophical study sometimes overlap, you may see connections not reflected in the "correct" answers, but if you can explain the connection, your answer may be correct.

1. Aren't people basically good?
2. Is there a God?
3. Do you believe in reincarnation?
4. Is homosexuality an inborn trait?
5. Do animals have the equivalent of human rights?
6. Is there a spirit world?
7. Does God really expect perfection?
8. Do you believe in evolution or creation?
9. Is it ever right to lie?
10. Is it ever right to kill?
11. Is the Bible the Word of God?
12. Is there more to life than this physical universe?
13. Do you believe in Heaven and Hell?
14. Do you believe in the Big Bang theory?
15. Do you believe that people are merely the product of their genes and their environment?

ANTHROPOLOGY

EPISTEMOLOGY

ONTOLOGY

COSMOLOGY

ETHICS

THEOLOGY

DEATH

HISTORY

Question Development

Now that you understand the terms, design five more question like the ones listed above and identify the assumption at work in each issue.

_____
_____
_____
_____
_____
_____
_____

Bible Study: 2 Peter 1:16–21

We looked at this passage when we were studying the inspiration of Scripture.
Now we will examine it more closely to see what it has to say about the
Christian epistemology (basis of knowledge, truth and authority).

1. Many critics of the Bible have accused the ancients of a simple-minded
   superstition which made them gullible to any sort of claim of divine or
   miraculous intervention in their lives. How does Peter respond to this
   charge in verse 16?

   _____

   _____

   _____

2. To what event in the life of Christ is Peter referring when he says that Jesus
   "received from God the Father, honor and glory"?

   _____

3. What word-picture does Peter use to describe the entrance of God's Word
   ("the prophetic word") into our lives?

   _____

   _____

   How is this word-picture similar to the story of "The Boys in The Box?"

   _____

   _____

   Has the Scripture ever provided light for you in a dark, difficult circum-
   stance? Describe a situation where you received guidance from Scripture.

   _____

   _____

4 Many people claim that the Bible can be interpreted to mean almost anything. What do you think it means when it says that "no prophecy of Scripture is of any private interpretation" (v. 20)?

_____

_____

5. According to verse 21, what was and what was not the source of the prophecy recorded in Scripture?

_____

_____

6. Does this claim of divine inspiration strengthen or weaken the Christian epistemology? Explain your answer.

_____

_____

_____

Read Chapter 7 and answer the following questions.

1. What is the "key tenet of naturalism"?

   _____

   _____

2. How does naturalist Sellars regard the Christian worldview? In his opinion, what has "rendered (Christianity) obsolete"?

   _____

   _____

3. How do Secular Humanists feel about the theology of the Cosmic Humanist?

   _____

   _____

4. What is the cosmology of the Secular Humanist? (Paraphrase the answers given in the book.)

   _____

   _____

5. For the naturalist, what is the ultimate means of perception?

   _____

   _____

6. Explain the "mind-body problem" of naturalism.

   _____

   _____

7. How does the naturalist's "monistic" view of the mind and body differ from the Christian's "dualistic" view?

_____

_____

8. What two troubling implications of the "mind-body problem" are discussed in the text?

_____

_____

9. Discussion question: So much about naturalism seems so hopeless and pessimistic, yet Secular Humanism is full of optimism about the future. Based on what we have read and discussed so far, what makes the humanist so optimistic?

_____

_____

Lecture Notes: Tension Points in Naturalism

This lecture overviews some of the problems which have surfaced in naturalism, problems which have been pointed out not just by critics of the view (such as theists) but by naturalists themselves.

I. Tension point one: Human Behavior — _____?

A. The premise:

1. Humans are _____, part of a _____
    _____which runs efficiently according to_____
    _____ principles. (Everything that happens is caused
    by something before it.)

2. Animals operate according to _____, without the
    capacity for _____.

B. The conclusion: Human behavior is controlled not by _____
    _____ but by external factors such as _____
    and _____. People have _____ in their
    behavior and are, therefore, _____ for their actions.

C. The effects: This assumption (that people are not responsible for
    their actions) affects the way a naturalist approaches disciplines such
    as _____ and _____.

II. Tension point two: Ethics — _____

    A. The premise: Science (the study of nature) can inform us about *is*
    (_____), but not about *ought* (how human
    animals ought to behave).

    B. The conclusion: Naturalism provides no _____ for ethics. There
    is nothing in nature to say that one behavior (_____an
    _____) is more or less righteous than another behavior
    (_____*for* a sick friend).

    C. The effects: Naturalists have a hard time when they speak of ethics.
    They speak of "moral" behavior and "the good life" without any way
    to define such terms. When they do speak of a basis for ethics, they
    cannot agree on what that basis is.

III. Tension point three: Epistemology — _____

    A. The premise: The human "mind" is the product of billions of years of
    _____ governed by _____.

    B. The conclusion: Human thinking can never be regarded as _____
    _____.

    C. The effect: _____
    ("I can be sure of _____, not even _____.")

Bible Study: Scripture on Naturalism

This brief study will show that the basic principles of naturalism are deeply contrary to the assumptions underlying a Christian worldview.

Part 1: Match the reference to the thought.

1. 2 Peter 3:3–7   a. the sovereignty of God
2. Hebrews 11:1–3   b. man's dominion over nature
3. Romans 1:18–20   c. nature: sufficient evidence for the existence of God
4. Amos 7:7–9   d. history interrupted by divine intervention
5. Psalm 8:3–8   e. creation out of nothing
6. Isaiah 14:24–27   f. cultures to be judged by an absolute standard

Part 2: Explain what the Scriptures listed above say about each of the statements listed below (basic assumptions of the naturalistic worldview):

- The history of the cosmos has been from the beginning an uninterrupted chain of cause-effect events.

- There is no evidence to support the notion of a Supreme Being who created the cosmos.

- In the absence of moral absolutes, each culture must determine its own moral code; no one code is superior to any other.

- History is controlled by blind, irrational chance.

- Man occupies no special place in the natural scheme of things.

- The cosmos is all that exists and is all that has ever existed.

Lecture Notes: Marxist Philosophy

I.   Overview: The differences between Secular Humanism and
     Marxism/Leninism are not so much differences in
     _____ both are _____ worldviews —
     but differences in _____ and _____.

A. Secular Humanists would see their atheistic agenda prevail through
    _____, _____, _____ and
    other _____.

B. Marxists look to _____ _____ to _____ the
    present system _____ _____ ___ _____ _____ society.

C. Because the two views are so similar, Christians find some of the same
    faults with both views:

    1. Both Secular Humanism and Marxism are _____ _____ about:

        a. _____ _____

        b. _____ _____ of creating a perfect _____ _____

    2. Both Secular Humanism and Marxism are blindly _____
        denying both the _____ and the _____
        of God.

II. Marxist view of reality (ontology):

A. _____ (_____ is all that exists)

B. Another way of saying _____ is all that exists (_____).

III. Marxist view of truth and knowledge (_____)

A. Ultimate confidence in _____, which is viewed as a
    virtually infallible _____ ____ _____.

B. No idea can be considered "_____" until it has been
    _____, _____ (thus denying the possibility of
    knowledge about the _____ _____).

IV. Marxist _____

    A. Views history as _____ _____, _____

       (_____)

    B. Process of historical development:

       1. Every established idea ("_____") is eventually opposed by
another idea ("_____").

       2. Eventually, a whole different way of thinking emerges
("_____"), which renders both thesis and antithesis _____.

       3. This synthesis eventually becomes _____, which is
opposed by _____ . . . and so forth without end.

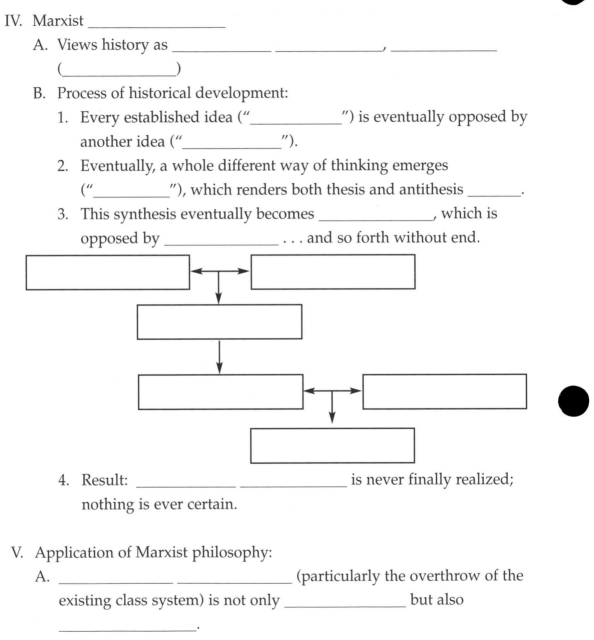

       4. Result: _____ _____ is never finally realized;
nothing is ever certain.

V. Application of Marxist philosophy:

    A. _____ _____ (particularly the overthrow of the
existing class system) is not only _____ but also

      _____.

    B. Anything which _____ such change is an _____

    to _____.

Bible Study: God and Nature

In naturalism, the cosmos is understood as a machine-like entity which oper ates independently of any outside force. The Bible portrays a very different picture of nature, as the careful work of the Creator who is vitally interested in His work. Listed below is a series of statements describing the cosmos (the ordered universe) as the naturalist understands it. Also listed are the references for eight passages of Scripture which specifically address the question of the relationship of God and nature. For each statement, list the reference(s) for the passages which speak(s) to the statement and briefly state the teaching of Scripture on that issue. (Some references will be used more than once, and some statements may have more that one reference related to them.)

1. Matter is self-existent, that is, it was not created but has always existed.

_____

_____

_____

2. The cosmos will always exist.

_____

_____

_____

3. The cosmos operates according to cause-effect principles, independent of outside forces. The physical principles which govern the operation of the cosmos arose spontaneously over time and are not the product of intelligent design and supervision.

_____

_____

_____

Genesis 1:1	Psalm 102:25–27	Psalm 104:10–30
John 1:1–3	Hebrews 11:3	Matthew 6:26–30
2 Peter 3:10–13	Revelation 21:1	

6 COSMIC HUMANIST AND BIBLICAL CHRISTIAN PHILOSOPHY

Read Chapter 9 and answer the following questions.

1. How do Cosmic Humanists feel about naturalism? Why?

_____

_____

_____

_____

2. What is "non-naturalism"?

_____

_____

_____

_____

3. Where does the Cosmic Humanist look to find truth?

_____

_____

_____

_____

4. Naturalism (Secular Humanism and Marxist Leninism) sees truth as objective facts, understood by reason. How does Cosmic Humanism understand truth?

_____

_____

_____

_____

5. The text uses the term "monism" to describe both the naturalist's and the Cosmic Humanist's concept of mind and brain. How does the term monism apply equally well to both?

_____

_____

_____

_____

6. Why do different cosmic Humanist thinkers express different interpretations of reality?

_____

_____

_____

_____

7. In Cosmic Humanism, what is the only substance which really exists?

_____

_____

_____

_____

Enrichment Activity: Letter from an Old Friend

Dear Melissa,

How are you doing? I know we haven't had much contact for a long time, but I just had to write to tell you about the most exciting thing that has happened to me! It has absolutely changed my life!

You know I never had much interest in religion. Even when you talked to me about Christianity, it didn't seem to be right for me. But I've found something so real, so exciting, that I just know it's what I've been looking for all my life!

It all started when a friend introduced me to a woman named Sophia. Sophia is into reading Tarot cards and that kind of thing. When Sophia asked if I would like her to read the cards for me, I said, "Sure ." (Actually, I was bored). I didn't pay much attention to her until she started telling me personal details about myself that only a close friend might know.

I asked my friend if she had told her about me. She said she had never told Sophia anything about me until she introduced us. Then Sophia went on to tell me more intimate things, secret thoughts I've never told anyone—secret ambitions, secret fears, even very specific ideas I've had about the kind of man I want to marry.

That was six months ago. Since then, I've learned to read the cards myself. Also, Sophia took me to see someone who was "channeling." I've never heard or seen anything like this! These people are onto something really spiritual and real!

I wish I could sit down with you in person and show you what I mean. I think you would see that Christianity is just a taste of the spiritual reality these people have opened up for me. I'd love to do the same thing for you! Everyone should know about this!

Write back. I'm anxious to hear what you have to say.

Betsy

How should Melissa respond to this letter? Should she go to see her friend or merely write back? What should she say in her response?

_____

_____

_____

_____

_____

_____

Read Chapter 10 and answer the following questions.

Introduction:

1. How do some Christians use Colossians 2:8 to support their belief that faith need not be defended on philosophical grounds? According to the text, what is wrong with this interpretation?

_____

_____

2. What led former atheist C. E. M. Joad "(to) gradually embrace the Christian view of the universe"?

_____

_____

Faith and Epistemology:

1. What does "faith precedes reason" mean? In what primary source of knowledge does the naturalist put his faith? In what primary source of knowledge does the Cosmic Humanist put his faith?

_____

_____

2. Christians are often accused of embracing a philosophy based not on fact but on superstition. According to the text, what is the basis of the Christian's "special revelation"?

_____

_____

3. What two principles are summarized in the last paragraph of the section "Faith and Epistemology"?

_____

_____

Bible Study: Evidence for Biblical Faith

Critics sometimes accuse the early Christians of blindly accepting the claims of Christ without sufficient evidence. In the New Testament, however, the truth about Jesus is cast in a far different light, with careful attention given to questions of evidence. As you answer the questions from the passages listed, notice how four different New Testament characters (Jesus, Paul, Peter and John the Apostle) explain their truth-claims in terms of hard evidence.

1. John 5:31–40

   Although Jesus could have laid out His claims in a dogmatic, take-it-or-leave-it approach, He was willing to discuss evidence supporting His claims. What four lines of evidence does Jesus cite to support His own testimony concerning Himself?

2. 1 Corinthians 15:12–19

   Some liberal Bible scholars have suggested that the Resurrection of Christ was an early Christian legend that was eventually enlarged into historical fact. They argue that the important thing was not whether Jesus actually rose from the dead but that the Christians believed in the doctrine of the Resurrection. How would the Apostle Paul have responded to such teaching? "If Christ is not risen," says Paul, several terrible implications would follow. What are they?

3. 2 Peter 1:16–18
   - How does Peter distinguish between the Christian message and "cunningly devised fables"?
   - When Peter says that he was an "eyewitness of His majesty," what event in the life of Christ does he have in mind?

4. 1 John 1:1–3

   John takes great pains to establish the fact that the Christian message is not the product of someone's theological speculation but of direct personal experience with Jesus Himself.
   - What three senses does John say were involved in his experience of Christ?
   - John uses repetition to emphasize points in his epistle. How many refer-ences to sense experience can you find in these three verses? List them.

Questions: "Doubting Thomases"

1. What limitations are placed on science?

   _____

   _____

   _____

   _____

2. What is the difference between science and scientism?

   _____

   _____

   _____

   _____

3. Why do secular worldviews claim science as their exclusive domain?

   _____

   _____

   _____

   _____

7 .... CHRISTIAN PHILOSOPHY

Lecture Notes: Scripture and Science

I. Limiting the _____:

   A. _____vs. _____

      1. Science is a _____ for investigating the

         _____.

      2. Naturalism is a _____ which depends solely

         on science for insights into _____ such as

         _____, _____, etc.

      3. Conclusion: There is no _____ _____ between

         scientific method and Biblical truth.

   B. Faith vs. Science

      1. Science and scientists are widely regarded as the final authority on

         everything, even on matters _____the realm of science

         (e.g., Carl Sagan's confident pronouncements on the origin of the

         cosmos).

      2. Some regard religious faith as a sort of primitive _____

         which is not a valid consideration in discussion of philosophical

         matters.

      3. Conclusion: When the authority of scientists is limited to their

         particular _____ and when religious faith is treated as

         an additional means of _____ _____ ,

         the field of controversy is reduced considerably.

II. The Remaining Controversies:

    A. Where the Bible is _____ , we should also be _____.
(e.g., on the age of the earth).

    B. Many controversies are not over scientific _____ but over
_____ _____ _____ _____. (People interpret
facts according to their worldview.)

    C. We should avoid the error of changing our _____ of
_____ to accommodate a current scientific theory. Science is a
rapidly changing discipline! A theory in vogue today may be hopelessly
_____ in fifty years!

Questions

Science and Christian Philosophy

1. How does the wise Christian philosopher regard science?

_____

_____

The Origin of Science

1. Why would a Marxist or Humanist worldview fail to "serve as a fitting base for modern science"?

_____

_____

2. Why does the author think Christianity provides a superior basis for scientific research?

_____

_____

Metaphysics: Ontology/Cosmology

1. In naturalism, matter is the ultimate reality. In Cosmic Humanism spirit is the ultimate reality. In Christianity, what is the ultimate reality?

_____

_____

2. What is the Christian view of the relationship between the natural and the supernatural? How does this view differ from that of the naturalist?

_____

_____

3. How do Christians understand the relationship between mind and matter? (How is this view different from the naturalist "materialist" view?)

_____

_____

Personal Manifesteo

Now that you have studied the basic worldview question, it is time for you to put your beliefs down on paper. You may have never had to answer questions like this before; but unless you spend the rest of your life in a monastery, you will have to deal with these questions again, either as you deal with your own doubts or as someone asks you a hard question about Christianity.

You may use any resource you choose in preparation for this assignment—a trusted counselor, a good book, the Bible, etc.—but your final project should be completed without the aid of any other resource except your Bible and perhaps some quotations.

Each question or set of questions should be answered in paragraph form. For each category, you should not only declare what you believe but also why you believe your answer to be true.

This project will be graded only on the basis of timely submission (with points off for late work) and evidence of a good-faith effort to answer the questions. Your instructor will read your manifesto in detail only if you request feedback. If you do not request feedback, your instructor will only scan your manifesto to insure that you have actually attempted to answer the questions.

1. What makes me think my world view is true and correct? (Epistemology)

2. How did everything begin? (Cosmology) How will everything end?

3. Is there a God? If so, what is God like? (Theology)

4. How can people best distinguish between good and evil? Is the difference between good and evil absolute (never changing) or relative (dependent upon the situation)? (Ethics)

5. What is man's relationship to the rest of the cosmos? Is man merely one species among many, or is there something special about man which sets him apart from the other creatures? (Anthropology)

6. What is man's basic moral nature? (Anthropology)

7. Who or what controls the course of events in the cosmos?

8. What happens to people after they die?

PARADIGM

∙∙∙ ●

Christianity

Epistemology	
Ontology	
Cosmology	
Ethics	
Anthropology	
Death	

CHART

	Naturalism (Secular Humanism, Marxism)	Cosmic Humanism (New Age)
Epistemology		
Ontology		
Cosmology		
Ethics		
Anthropology		
Death		

Introduction to Ethics

I.   Where do moral values come from?

_____

_____

_____

II. How are moral values known?

_____

_____

_____

III. Are moral values absolute or relative?

_____

_____

_____

IV. What is the highest good?
  A. Hedonism: _____

  B. Pragmatism/Utilitarianism: _____

  C. Legalism: _____

  D. Situation Ethics: _____

  E. Cultural Relativism: _____

Read Chapter 11. For each statement, write **True** or **False** according to the Secular Humanists quoted. For each answer, give the name of the Humanist whose quote you used, along with the first few words of the quote. (Note: Use only direct quotes, not indirect quotes, summaries or interpretations by someone else.)

_____ 1. Secular Humanists reject the unchanging moral codes of religious systems. _____

_____

_____ 2. Secular Humanists regard morality and ethics as an important part of their philosophy. _____

_____

_____ 3. Secular Humanists agree on most ethical issues. _____

_____

_____ 4. Secular Humanists have no unchanging standard which requires people to behave in a certain way. _____

_____

_____ 5. Secular Humanists cannot finally agree whether the absence of God from their ethics means that ethics is relative or if it means that some other basis for absolute ethics must exist.

_____

_____

_____ 6. Some Secular Humanists appeal to reason as the final test of morality. _____

_____

_____ 7. Some Secular Humanists appeal to biology (survival of the fittest) as the final test of morality. _____

_____

_____ 8. Some Secular Humanists hold to situation ethics. _____

_____

_____ 9. Secular Humanists hold to a pragmatic approach to ethics.

_____

NON-CHRISTIAN ETHICS

Lecture Notes

I. Basic Principles

   A. Each person is _____.

   B. Therefore:

      1. Moral values are sourced in _____.

      2. _____ moral values are rejected.

II. Implication: "Boundless Ethical Relativism"

   A. People can _____ moral values.

   B. People can _____ about moral values
they once _____.

   C. No one can evaluate someone else's _____.

   D. Ultimately, there is no real difference between _____
and _____.

ETHICAL SYSTEMS

	Secular Humanism	Marxism/ Leninism	Cosmic Humanism	Biblical Christianity
Source of Moral Values				
How Moral Values Are Known				
Relativity of Moral Values				
Highest Good				

Quiz

Answer these true/false statements. You may use Scripture, but be sure to make a note of the passage you used to arrive at your answer.

_____ 1. Evil is the exact opposite of good.

_____ 2. Satan is the eternal enemy of God.

_____ 3. Good could not exist without evil.

_____ 4. Evil could not exist without good.

_____ 5. The basis of Christian ethics is the character of God.

_____ 6. Every evil deed is merely a perversion of a good deed.

_____ 7. Evil has always existed.

_____ 8. Evil will always exist.

_____ 9. Moral values are sourced in man.

_____ 10. Moral values are sourced outside of man.

_____ 11. Conscience is a source of moral values.

_____ 12. Conscience is a totally reliable source of moral values.

_____ 13. The Scriptures are a source of moral values.

_____ 14. The life of Christ is a source of moral values.

_____ 15. The Scriptures are a more reliable source of moral values than the conscience.

_____ 16. The conscience is a more reliable source of moral values than the Scriptures.

_____ 17. Moral values are revealed most clearly in the conscience.

_____ 18. Moral values are revealed most clearly in the Scriptures.

_____ 19. Moral values are revealed most clearly in the life of Christ.

_____ 20. Without the knowledge of evil, we would never be able to appreciate the holiness of God.

Lecture Notes: Christian Ethics Based on the Character of God

I. First implication: Evil is only good perverted.
  A. Everything God created is good; evil is only an ugly parody of the good.

  _____

  _____

  B. Evil is not the opposite of good any more than cold is the
    opposite of heat.

  _____

  _____

  C. The origin of evil: the rebellion.

  _____

  _____

II. Second implication: Moral values can be known both by intuition and by
  revelation.
  A. First level: Morality is inscribed on the conscience, but imperfectly.
    (Romans 2:14–15, Proverbs 14:12)

  _____

  _____

  B. Second level: Morality is revealed more fully in Scripture.
    (Deuteronomy 29.29, Ex 20.1-17)

  _____

  _____

  C. Third level: Morality is revealed consummately in Christ.
    (John 1:14–18)

  _____

  _____

ETHICAL SYSTEMS

	Secular Humanism	Marxism/Leninism	Cosmic Humanism	Biblical Christianity
Source of Evil				
Source of Moral Values				
How Moral Values Are Known				
Relativity of Moral Values				
Highest Good				

Case Study in Ethics

Bob could hear his father's words ringing in his ears, "Get those grades up or else!" Easy for him to say. He'd never had one of Mr. Beaker's chemistry tests. Today' quiz was the last grade before mid-term reports.

As he finished, he checked his answers twice. A bad grade here would be curtains at home. He had promised his father his grades would improve. He had even prayed about his chemistry grade in front of his father. Even though Dad was not a Christian, he was willing to let Bob do anything to improve his chemistry grade. Now was the chance to show Dad that prayer really works!

Mr. Beaker was having the students grade their own quizzes today. As Mr. Beaker began to read through the answer key, Bob's eyes glanced ahead a few questions. To his shock, he saw that he had reversed two answers—to questions he knew cold! How could he have made such a mistake? If he hurried, he could change the answers before Mr. Beaker got to those questions. What should he do? What's at stake?

Philosophical Issues in Biology

	Origin of Life	Development of Life	Man's Place in Natural Order
Secular Humanism			
Marxism			
Cosmic Humanism			
Biblical Christianity			

Read Chapter 15 (Conclusion section first) and answer the following questions.

1. What are the six "planks" that form the basis for the Humanist's case for evolution?

2. Why is the word "supernatural" a meaningless concept in Humanism?

3. Why does the author say that neither creationism nor evolution is "strictly scientific"?

4. In his book *He Is There and He is Not Silent*, Francis Schaeffer argued that there are only a few possible explanations for the origin of life:

   Everything came from nothing.
   Everything came from an impersonal source.
   Everything came from a personal source.

   Which option would the Secular Humanist choose? What problem does the author see with this view?

5. What is the author's criticism of the evolutionary theory of natural selection?

6. What two problems does the author see with notion of the "survival of the fittest"?

7. What is there about the fossil record which made it necessary for evolutionists to resort to the "punctuated equilibrium" theory?

8. What other applications for evolution does the Humanist see besides biology?

Read Chapter 17 and answer the following questions.

1. What is surprising about the Cosmic Humanist's biology?

_____

_____

_____

_____

_____

2. How is the Cosmic Humanist's view of evolution different from the Secular Humanist's and Marxist's view?

_____

_____

_____

_____

_____

3. Study the quote from John White about the final appearance of Christ. How is White's version of the Second Coming different from the one described in the New Testament?

_____

_____

_____

_____

_____

Philosophical Issues in Biology

	Origin of Life	Development of Life	Man's Place in Natural Order
Secular Humanism			
Marxism			
Cosmic Humanism			
Biblical Christianity			

Psychological Worldviews Diagnostic Chart

	Secular Humanism	Marxism	Cosmic Humanism	Biblical Christianity
Nature of reality: monism/ dualism				
Human Nature				
Personal responsibility in society/ reason for evil				
Guilt				

Psychological Worldviews Diagnostic Chart *(cont'd.)*

	Secular Humanism	Marxism	Cosmic Humanism	Biblical Christianity
Solution to man's need				
The future				
Authority				
Freedom				
Suffering				

Read Chapter 19 and answer the following questions.

1. Why do humanists reject Behaviorism and Freudianism?

   _____

   _____

   _____

   _____

   _____

2. For a humanist, all men are basically good. Is society as a whole good?

   _____

   _____

3. The humanist transforms self-centeredness into a virtue. True or False?

   _____

4. What psychologist is associated with the concept "self-actualization?"
   What does this term mean?

   _____

   _____

5. According to the humanists, who is the highest authority on values and ethics?

   _____

   _____

6. What are the three major assumptions of Humanist Psychology?

   _____

   _____

Lecture Notes: Introduction to Marxist/Leninist Psychology

As we have seen in the study of other disciplines, Marxist/Leninist thinking is closely aligned with _____ ideas. The same is true in psychology.

I. Marxist/Leninist tie to _____

   A. Behaviorism views man as simply a _____ which can be predetermined to respond in a particular way to a certain set of circumstances or stimuli. (S – R)

   B. Two important names:

      1. B. F. Skinner — psychologist (traditional behaviorist)

         "_____" of the year 1972. Saw man as strictly _____ in nature. All human behavior had strictly physical causes. Control the _____ and you control the _____. Problem — eliminates free will.

      2. Ivan Pavlov — early twentieth century Russian psychologist. Attempted to reconcile _____ (naturalism) with the _____ dialect. Famous for experiments with ringing bells while feeding _____ which caused a salivating response when only the _____ was present. Experiments on conditioned reflexes led him to believe man could be conditioned to make only good responses and therefore man was

         _____.

II. Behaviorism's conflict with _____

   A. Strict behaviorism views man as _____. Fits somewhat with evolutionary model of natural forces shaping man and the Marxist belief that _____ is inevitable.

   B. But the revolution to bring about the communism requires men to actively _____ to bring it about. Strict behaviorism denies the free will necessary to bring this about. Men can change circumstances to shape an _____ that will shape men into the _____ society.

   C. Marxists point out that _____ — man's second receptor system allows him to transmit and receive stimuli that go beyond Pavlov's bells.

III. Dialectical Behavior

   A. The individual's freedom (_____) struggles with man's behavioristic tendencies (_____) to bring about the new social order (_____).

   B. The dialectal view of behavior is seen as the only _____ view.

IV. Conclusion

   A. Marxist freedom is only the opportunity for the individual to choose what kind of society will determine his behavior. Individual freedom is _____.

   B. Marxist's order results in loss of both man's _____ and _____.

Psychology Worldviews Applied

Analyze each scenario from the humanist and Biblical worldviews. How would the actions of the individual be interpreted by each view? What actions would be recommended? What results could you anticipate?

A. Erin comes from a broken home in a low socio-economic neighborhood. She is often embarrassed at school because her clothes are not as attractive as other students. While shopping at the mall she tries on a new outfit that she longs to own. Since she doesn't have enough money for the purchase, she puts her own clothes on over the new outfit and tries to leave the store. She is caught and arrested. She is released to her mom and sent to a first-offender counseling program.

B. Robert and Angie have been dating six months. They believe that one day they will marry. Robert begins to pressure Angie towards sexual involvement. Angie has been taught the traditional Biblical values including virginity until marriage. It seems many of their friends are sexually involved and Angie feels guilty for not meeting Robert's "need" in this way. She finally gives in believing that one day they will be married anyway. Afterwards she experiences intense feelings of guilt. She is very uncomfortable attending church. Robert says her personality has changed and she is not as much fun anymore. He considers breaking off their relationship but agrees to go see a counselor first.

C. Jason's work situation is very discouraging. He works long hours and carries a full load at school. His boss, Attila, never expresses appreciation and has not given Jason a raise in months. Attila's belittling remarks about Jason's work and appearance seem unwarranted. Jason would like to quit but he needs the money for school bills. Jason begins to steal money from work and rationalizes it on the basis of his lack of a long overdue raise. He sees no reason to put up with this hassle without appropriate reenumeration. He begins to feel bad about himself and his actions. He reads a newspaper advice columnist and concludes that his problem is low self-esteem as a result of Attila's continued badgering. He goes to a counselor to get help with his problem.

Scenario Analysis

	Secular Humanism	Biblical Christianity	Marxism (optional)	Cosmic Humanism (optional)
Problem:				
Source or Cause:				
Solution/ Action:				
Anticipated Result:				

Psychological Worldviews Diagnostic Chart

	Secular Humanism	Marxism	Cosmic Humanism	Biblical Christianity
Nature of reality: monism/dualism				
Human Nature				
Personal responsibility in society/reason for evil				
Guilt				

Psychological Worldviews Diagnostic Chart *(cont'd.)*

	Secular Humanism	Marxism	Cosmic Humanism	Biblical Christianity
Solution to man's need				
The future				
Authority				
Freedom				
Suffering				

Read Chapter 23. In each quotation circle the words that you believe to be the most powerful. Which words carry the most "clout"?

1. Eric From: ". . . the social process . . . creates man. Just as primitive man was helpless before natural forces, modern man is helpless before the social and economic forces created by himself."

2. Lawrence Castler: " . . . marriage and family life have been largely responsible, I suggest, for today's prevailing neurotic climate with its pervasive insecurity, and it is precisely this climate that makes so difficult the acceptance of a different healthier way of life."

3. Sol Gordon: "The traditional family with all its supposed attributes, enslaved woman; it reduced her to a breeder and caretaker of children, a servant to her spouse, a cleaning lady, and at times a victim of the labor market as well."

(Assignment for Day 2)

Questions To Consider

1. Keep the following questions in mind while reading the Introduction, Conclusion, Church, Education and Family sections of Chapter 24.

    *   Why are religion and the church an enemy of the revolution?

    _____

    _____

    _____

    _____

    *   Why does the family become not only unnecessary but a liability for the Marxist?

    _____

    _____

    _____

    _____

2. Throughout the week look for examples of common social problems and proposed solutions found in newspaper articles, editorials, letters to the editor, news magazines, other media, etc. Bring them in on Day 4.

    _____

    _____

    _____

    _____

Lecture Notes

I. Economic Determinism

   A. Social consciousness and organization are tied to _____

      _____ _____.

   B. The _____ unit is an important part of _____ economic production.

   C. As we _____ higher toward socialism the traditional family is an outmoded _____ entity. It actually retards progress toward the true _____ society.

   D. Mode of Economic Production:

      social/relational patterns → social norms → political/legal norms

II. The Inevitability of "Scientific" _____

   A. The Marxist sees himself as holding the most _____ of worldviews.

   B. Progress toward the true communist utopia is rooted in the scientific _____ of evolution.

   C. Man is evolving not only _____ but also _____.

III. The Church

   A. The church is an _____ of the revolution.

   B. The church _____ the workers (proletariat) and preserves outmoded social norms and values that are based on _____ and not _____.

IV. The Proletariat and Human Freedom

    A. The _____ is shaped by the force of society.

    B. One group of men — _____ — is able to under-
stand these forces and rises above them choosing to remodel society.

    C. Ultimately, when _____ resistance has been broken,
this remodeling will produce a communist utopia where no
_____ will be necessary.

SOCIAL ORGANIZATION

Case Study: China's One-Child Policy

One attempt to apply Marxist Sociological theory is the One-Child Policy advocated by the communist Chinese government in China in the early 1980's. This dramatic shift away from the traditional large family model was taken as a major social and economic challenge. The factory town of Changzhou was held up as an exemplary model town. The planning council determined the number of births permitted each year. Monitoring of pregnancy and contraception took place through the factory as well as by the neighborhood population control workers.

Couples were required to have a permit to try for their initial pregnancy. The permit card was necessary to receive free pre-natal care and for registering the child's birth at the police station. If pregnancy occurred without permission, the worker lost bonus pay and model worker status. They would be continuously pressured to have an abortion which was provided at no charge.

Once the child was born, the mother was encouraged to take out a "one-child" certificate or "Glory Certificate" to promise to only have one child. This certificate resulted in an additional three months maternity leave at full pay, and many other benefits. The child was entitled to $30.00 per month from the government, free education, priority for university placement, and priority for job placement. If 100% of mothers in the factory took the one-child pledge, the factory was granted model factory status and all workers received a bonus.

Free child care was provided in the factory along with free medical checkups. If the couple had a second pregnancy and refused to have an abortion, they were required to pay back the cost of all these benefits and would suffer a wage cut at the factory. Opportunities for jobs or improved housing were also reduced.

Ceremonies and public rallies were held regularly to recognize success in the family planning effort. The factory—the basic unit of production—replaced the family as the provider of child care and education. Children were taught songs to support the government goal with lyrics such as "We don't want any brothers or sisters, we are all happy, mother had only me."

Responding to the "one-child" call of the government was to become more important than any other family priority (such as the preservation of the family line or name). The good of the country was valued over family preferences. Goal-setting, rewards, and government services were all delivered through the factory. This drastic realignment of cultural priorities was praised by Marxists and humanists as far-sighted government planning and enlightened leadership.

Sociology Worldviews Overview

	Secular Humanist	Marxist/ Leninist	Biblical Christianity
Individual free will/ responsibility:			
Origin of family, church, state:			
Dignity of the individual:			

WORLDVIEW PERSPECTIVES

	Secular Humanism	Marxism/ Leninism	Cosmic Humanism	Biblical Christianity
Origin:	man's idea evolved			God-ordained
Value:	blocks self-actualization		outdated	
FAMILY PROBLEMS:		indicate family has evolved behold being effective		

WORLDVIEW PERSPECTIVES

	Secular Humanism	Marxism/ Leninism	Cosmic Humanism	Biblical Christianity
Women's Rights:	feminism		free women from old roles	
Marital fidelity, sexual morality:		free sexual expression		holy, sacred
Right to depart from traditional values/ patterns:	man made it, man can change it		change is necessary to reach higher self	

Read the last half of Chapter 27 and answer the following questions.

1. If man is the source of his own standards, which men will determine morality and law?

   _____

   _____

   _____

   _____

   _____

   _____

   _____

2. Are these morals, laws and rights absolute and constant?

   _____

   _____

   _____

   _____

   _____

   _____

3. Thought question: Under positive law, what is left to control the state to prevent those in authority from abusing their power?

   _____

   _____

   _____

   _____

   _____

The Declaration of Independence

In Congress, July 4, 1776,
the Unanimous Declaration of
the Thirteen United States of America

When in the course of human events, it becomes necessary for one people to dissolve the political bands which have connected them with another, and to assume among the Powers of the earth, the separate and equal station to which the [1]Laws of Nature and of [2]Nature's God entitle them, a decent respect to the opinions of mankind requires that they should declare the causes which impel them to the separation.

We hold these truths to be [3]self-evident, that all men are [4]created equal, that they are endowed by their [5]Creator with certain unalienable rights, that among these are Life, Liberty and the pursuit of Happiness. That to [6]secure these rights, Governments are instituted among Men, deriving their just [7]powers from the consent of the governed. That whenever any Form of Government becomes destructive of these ends, it is the Right of the People to alter or to abolish it, [8]and to institute new Government, laying its foundation on such principles and organizing its powers in such form, as to them shall seem most likely to effect their Safety and Happiness.

Compare the humanist thinking to the ideas expressed in the Declaration of
Independence.

HUMANIST	#	DECLARATION OF INDEPENDENCE
_____	1	_____
_____	2	_____
_____	3	_____
_____	4	_____
_____	5	_____
_____	6	_____
_____	7	_____
_____	8	_____

Enrichment Activity: Berman: Religion and Law

Prior to World War I, and into the 1920's America professed itself to be a Christian country. Even two generations ago, if one had asked Americans where our Constitution— or, indeed, our whole concept of law—came from, on what it was ultimately based, the overwhelming majority would have said, "the Ten Commandments," or "the Bible," or perhaps "the law of God." John Adams' conception that our law is rooted in a common religious tradition was shared not only by the Protestant descendants of the English settlers on this continent and their black slaves, but also by tens of millions of immigrants from Western and Southern and Eastern Europe, a large proportion of whom were Roman Catholics and Jews. Indeed, throughout the entire nineteenth and into the early twentieth century, America studied its law chiefly from Blackstone, who wrote that "[the] law of nature . . . dictated by God himself . . . is binding . . . in all countries and at all times; no human laws are of any validity if contrary to this; and such of them as are valid derive all their force, and all their authority, mediately or immediately, from this original."

Within the past two generations the public philosophy of America has shifted radically from a religious to a secular theory of law, from a moral to a political or instrumental theory, and from a communitarian to an individualistic theory. Law is now generally considered—at least in public discourse—to be essentially a pragmatic device for accomplishing specific political, economic, and social objectives. Its tasks are thought to be finite, material, impersonal— to get things done, to make people act in certain ways. Rarely, if ever, does one hear it said that law is a reflection of an objective justice or of the ultimate meaning or purpose of life. Usually it is thought to reflect, at best, the community's sense of what is useful.

Juris #1
Berman, H. J., *Religion and Law: The First Amendment in Historical Perspective*, pages 11–13.
Originally published in the *Emory Law Journal*, Volume 35, No. 4 (Fall 1986).

Questions: Berman: Religion and Law

1. Does Berman agree with the notion that, prior to 1920, the Biblical view of natural law was held by very few people?

_____

_____

_____

_____

2. What ideas expressed by Blackstone are contrary to the idea of positive law?

_____

_____

_____

_____

3. Berman describes a shift in legal philosophy using three comparisons. Identify and explain. What are the implications of these ideas when applied?

_____

_____

_____

_____

Note: Law has become a tool for use by those in power to reshape society. This promotes an agenda in a pragmatic way to move the cultural environment toward a desired end. The humanist utilized this view of law to remodel society to allow man's inner goodness to flourish. Men are not ruled by law rooted in the absolute truth of the character of God. Rather, man uses law for his own ends, even to attempt to eradicate the concept of God from public view.

13

Good Law Is Limiting

Good law is limiting. It prevents the exercise of arbitrary power by the state and its agencies. If, however, the foundation undergirding law in a Christian society shifts from a Christian to a humanistic base (legal positivism), then a "nervous breakdown" occurs. Anarchy may result, and, if it does, history teaches us that an imposed order will be inevitable.

John Whitehead
The Second American Revolution,
Crossway Books, 1988, page 80.

1. "Good law is limiting." Why?

   _____

   _____

   _____

2. "It prevents the exercise of arbitrary power by the state and its agencies." Why?

   _____

   _____

   _____

3. "If, however, the foundation undergirding law in a Christian society shifts from a Christian to a humanist base (legal positivism), then a 'nervous breakdown' occurs." Why?

   _____

   _____

   _____

4. "Anarchy may result, and, if it does, history teaches us that an imposed order will be inevitable." Why?

   _____

   _____

Biblical Brainstorm

Malachi 2:9	Matthew 5:21–22
1 Timothy 5:21	Acts 5:1–4
Exodus 22:9	Ephesians 4:28
Ezra 7:26	Exodus 20:13–16
Acts 10:34–35	Romans 13:1–4
Galatians 3:28	Acts 17:31
James 2:1–7	Deuteronomy 1:17
Isaiah 1:16–17	Leviticus 19:15
1 Timothy 5:8	

Principles

_____

_____

_____

_____

_____

_____

_____

_____

_____

_____

_____

_____

_____

_____

_____

_____

Read Chapter 29 and answer the following questions.

1. Where do Cosmic Humanists look for standards of law?

   _____

   _____

2. Who becomes the ultimate authority?

   _____

   _____

3. Gawain is concerned about people suppressing _____

   _____.

4. This "internal guidance system" is contrasted with_____

   _____.

5. Compare with Romans 1:18. What is suppressed here?

   _____

   _____

   _____

   _____

6. What are the anticipated results of each suppression?

   _____

   _____

   _____

   _____

Bible References for Comparison

Zechariah 8:16 _____

_____

Romans 1:20–25 _____

_____

John 8:32 _____

_____

Judges 21:25 _____

_____

Romans 2:2 _____

_____

Genesis 3 _____

_____

1 Samuel 13, 15 _____

_____

Positive Law	Topic	Biblical Law
	Origin of law	
	Role of government	
	Courts	
	Source of human rights	
	Power of the state	
	Final authority	
	Justice	
	Exercise of rights	
	Future judgment/ accountability	

Read Chapter 32 and answer the following questions.

1. The Marxist believes all social and political structure is determined by the _____ structures of the society.

2. The Marxist believes that capitalism always exploits the citizens and is therefore intolerable. True or False?

3. How would Marxists rank the following, with 1 being the ideal and 4 the least tolerable:
   _____ capitalism
   _____ no state at all
   _____ socialism
   _____ communism

4. To bring about the transition from capitalism to communism, all means of production must shift from private ownership to the hands of the

   _____.

5. Lenin saw the state as "a special organization of _____."

6. Demonstration of force and oppression are necessary and desirable activities of the state according to Lenin. True or False?

7. The Marxist believes dictatorship of the Party is synonymous with dictatorship of _____.

8. To the Marxist, the state is eternal. True or False?

9. World communism is a goal of the Marxist. True or False?

10. Use of violence and oppression are acceptable means of realizing Marxist goals. True or False?

15 THE STATE: ORDAINED BY GOD OR PRODUCT OF EVOLUTION?

Lecture Notes: Major Ideas

I. Economic Determinism

   A. The _____ of a society is the foundation of the society.

   B. Control of the means of _____ must be shifted from _____ control to _____ control.

   C. If the existing government encourages a _____ economy it must be overthrown and replaced with a _____ system which is more _____ and less _____ of the proletariat.

II. The State

   A. The state is a necessary _____ which is always a tool of _____ for one class over another.

   B. The state is useful in bringing about the transition from _____ to _____.

   C. Social _____ and the use of _____ will be necessary in this transition to _____ the opposition by the bourgeoisie.

   D. _____ by the state is necessary to keep bourgeoisie from regaining power.

III. The Party

    A. The dictatorship of the Marxist/Leninist _____ is synonymous with the dictatorship of the _____.

    B. The Party must guide the _____.

    C. People opposed to the Party are _____ of the state and must be _____.

IV. Ultimate Goals

    A. Theoretically, the _____ withers away.

    B. Although the new world _____ and the withering away of the _____ are an inevitable evolutionary state, _____ _____ is the immediate goal as the next step in the process.

V. Marxist Means to State Ends

    A. Those who oppose the goals of the revolution must be _____.

    B. Marxists have historically utilized all means of violence and oppression to bring about the revolution. As a result, over _____ people have been slaughtered. Active persecution of _____ and the _____ has always been a part of the Marxist agenda.

15 THE STATE: ORDAINED BY GOD OR PRODUCT OF EVOLUTION?

Bible Study: Politics

How does the Biblical worldview of the origin and purpose of the state differ from the non-Biblical views?

Romans 13:1–4 _____

_____

1 Timothy 2:1–3 _____

_____

Exodus 18:13–26 _____

_____

1 Peter 2:13–14 _____

_____

Psalm 103:19 _____

_____

Daniel 6; Acts 14:18–19 _____

_____

Judges 21:25 _____

_____

Proverbs 16:10–13 _____

_____

Proverbs 20:26 _____

_____

Proverbs 22:11; Proverbs 25:4–5 _____

_____

Proverbs 29:2 _____

_____

Proverbs 29:4 _____

_____

Proverbs 29:14 _____

_____

Proverbs 24:23–25 _____

_____

Proverbs 21:1 _____

_____

Proverbs 31:8–9 _____

_____

Proverbs 31:3–5 _____

_____

Lecture Notes: Major Ideas

I. Mankind is evolving to a higher collective _____ which tran-
    scends all _____ and _____ boundaries.

II. The _____ vision includes the awareness of the unity of all
    of _____.

III. Mankind's evolution is not just _____, but one of a total
     _____ development. We can cultivate this _____
     and accelerate the process.

IV. As each person develops this consciousness, they will be _____
    _____. (Compare Judges 21:25.) The need for political form
    or limits will _____ _____.

V. All other _____ must be abandoned. _____ and
    its claim of absolute _____ must be eliminated to enhance
    the coming of the Planetary Age.

Socialism

Definition: Socialism is an economic system based on the abolition of private ownership of the means of production.

Pro Socialism	Against Socialism
_____	_____

Pro Guaranteed Income   Against Guaranteed Income

16 JUSTICE, THE FALL AND THE STEWARDSHIP OF RESOURCES

Read Chapter 36 and answer the following questions.

1. According to Marx, the key problem with capitalism is that is breeds

   _____.

2. What two flaws were attributed to capitalism by Karl Marx?
   1) _____
   2) _____

3. The destruction of capitalism and victory of the proletariat is ultimately
   guaranteed by the _____.

4. The first phase of communism is _____.

5. The first phase of the transition to communism will involve taking
   _____ from its rightful owners.

6. Lenin recognized the necessity of some capitalism in the gradual process
   toward communism. True or False?

7. In the inevitable worldwide communist utopia, government will be
   unnecessary. True or False?

Quotations

"Communism, as described by a Marxist, refers to an economic system based on socialism, in which no classes exist and everyone works according to his ability and receives according to his need." David Noebel

"The theory of communists may be summed up in a single sentence: Abolition of private property." Karl Marx

"Communist society means that everything—the land, the factories—is owned in common. Communism means working in common." V. I. Lenin

"The economic basis of the new world order must be the establishment of a unified planned system of economy." Georgi Shakhnazaron

"If the market is not allowed to steer the whole economic apparatus, the government must do it." Ludwig von Mises

"It is no longer the consumers, but the government who decides what should be produced and in what quantity and quality." Ludwig von Mises

Lecture Notes: Points of Emphasis in Marxist Economics

I. The _____ System Is Flawed

    A. If one group accumulates _____, it means another group
        automatically accumulates _____ and _____. It
        is as if the amount of wealth is constant. Capitalist economic thinkers
        view the potential of creating new wealth and growth so that one man's
        _____ is not automatically another man's _____.

    B. Capitalist economies operate at the whim of _____ _____
        while a socialist economy is _____ _____. A capitalist
        economist believes _____ _____ forces provide more
        opportunity for everyone and that _____ controlled
        economics are ineffective.

II. The Dialectic (Thesis — _____ — Synthesis)
    The destruction of capitalism and the victory of the _____
    is ultimately guaranteed by the _____.

III. The Transition to _____

    A. Capitalism — _____ — Communism

    B. The abolishment of _____ _____ will be

        _____.

    C. Engels describes the final phase, pure communism, in this way.
        "Finally, when all capital, all production, and all exchange are concen-
        trated in the hands of the nation, _____ _____ will
        automatically have ceased to exist, _____ will have become
        superfluous, and _____ will have so increased and men
        will be so much changed that the last forms of the old _____
        _____ will also be able to fall away."

IV. Conclusion

    A. The final phase of ultimate _____ _____ has
        yet to be realized in any society.

    B. Instead of universal _____, the redistribution of
        _____ in communist economies has resulted in low produc-
        tion, shortages of man's basic supplies and in many cases a lower
        _____ _____ _____.

Enrichment Activity: Letter to the Editor

April 15

Dear Editor:

I am a graduate student in economics at EDBD University. I just paid my taxes and it is frustrating to see how this economy works. The rich get all the breaks. It would be great if there were no rich and no poor, if (1) everyone had the same amount of money. Wouldn't it be a more just and fair society if everyone had the same amount of wealth? It would (2) eliminate social discord among various groups and everyone would respect each other more.

(3) If we had a central planning board to regulate big business it would make things more fair, too. Wouldn't this result in more freedom and justice for all?

(4) I suppose it won't change right away. The rich will get richer which automatically means the poor will have less. Perhaps the free market economy doesn't work after all.

Sincerely,

I. M. Poor
Graduate Student
EDBD University

Response to Letter to the Editor

	Major Idea	Possible response
(1)		
(2)		
(3)		
(4)		

Quotation

"Put bluntly, the Christian view of economics is less concerned with money that it is with freedom, justice, and responsibility. Money does not make any person more human or closer to conformity to Christ's image. But economic systems that check injustice and grant men responsibility—in terms both of private property and economic decisions—can allow men the freedom to act with all the dignity of beings created in God's image. This, according to the Christian view, is the important end of economic theory: offering men not riches or luxury but the freedom to seek fulfillment through understanding their role in God's scheme of things."

David Noebel
Understanding the Times

Part One

Read Chapter 42, Introduction through Resurrection in History, and answer the following questions.

1. What reasons does Noebel give for the trustworthiness of the Bible as a historical document?

    _____

    _____

    _____

    _____

2. The Christian believes the outcome of history is assured. True or False?

    _____

    _____

    _____

    _____

3. The Christian believes God made the world but is not actively involved in the flow of history. True or False?

    _____

    _____

    _____

    _____

4. The only references to Jesus in history are those found in the Bible. True or False?

    _____

5. According to the Bible, man's experience with God is not just in his head or "inner life," but in space/time history. True or False?

    _____

    _____

    _____

    _____

Bible Study

What do these Scripture passages teach us about history? Write your findings as generalizations, avoiding specific details.

a. Genesis 1:1; John 1:1–5

_____

_____

b. Proverbs 21:1, 8:15–16; Daniel 4:17, 5:18–23

_____

_____

c. 1 Corinthians 10:1–11; Deuteronomy 7:17–19; Daniel 5:18–23

_____

_____

d. Hosea 13:16; Joel 3:1–8, 12, 19; Genesis 18:17–18

_____

_____

e. Obadiah 15; Matthew 24:14; 2 Peter 3:10–11; Revelation 21:1; 1 John 2:3

_____

_____

f. Romans 13:1–4

_____

_____

g. 2 Kings 17:6–18; Isaiah 10:5, 12, 24–27; Acts 4:27–28, 2:22–23, Genesis 50:20

_____

_____

h. Romans 8:28, 11:33–36; Isaiah 55:8–11; Deuteronomy 29:29

_____

_____

i. Psalm 103:19; Ephesians 1:9–11; Acts 17–26; 1 Timothy 6:14–15

_____

_____

Part Two

Read the remainder of Chapter 42 and answer the following questions.

1. What gives history purpose?

   _____

   _____

   _____

   _____

2. History is linear. What does this mean?

   _____

   _____

   _____

   _____

3. It has been said that all of history is redemptive history. To what do
   followers of each worldview look for redemption?

   _____

   _____

   _____

   _____

   _____

   _____

   _____

Quotation

God is the Lord of history. This is clearly taught in Scripture. Old Testament writers affirmed that God's kingdom rules over all (Psalm 103:19), even over the kingdoms of the nations (2 Chronicles 20:6), and that He turns the heart of the king wherever He wishes (Proverbs 21:1). New Testament writers tell us that God accomplishes all things according to the counsel of His will (Ephesians 1:11), and that He has determined the times set for the nations of the earth and the exact places where they should live (Acts 17:26).

This means, as Ladd puts it, that "God is King and acts in history to bring history to a divinely directed goal." God is in control of history. This does not mean that He manipulates men as if they were puppets; man's freedom to make his own decisions and his responsibility for those decisions are at all times maintained. But it does mean that God overrules even the evil deeds of men so as to make them serve His purpose. An outstanding Old Testament illustration of this is found in the story of Joseph. After Joseph's brothers had sold him into slavery, Joseph became the chief ruler of Egypt under Pharaoh, and was thus instrumental in preserving many, including his own family, from famine. The words with which he addressed his brothers after his father's death underscore God's sovereign lordship over history: "As for you, you meant evil against me; but God meant it for good, to bring it about that many people should be kept alive, as they are today" (Genesis 50:20). The supreme New Testament illustration of God's sovereign control over history is, of course, the crucifixion of Jesus Christ. Though unquestionably the most wicked deed in history, even this terrible crime was completely under God's control: "For truly in this city there were gathered together against thy servant Jesus, whom thou didst anoint, both Herod and Pontius Pilate, with the Gentiles and the people of Israel, to do whatever thy hand and thy plan had predestined to take place" (Acts 4:27–38). Precisely because of God's control, the most accursed deed in history became the heart of God's redemptive plan and the supreme source of blessing to mankind. As the author of Psalm 76 puts it, "Surely the wrath of men shall praise thee" (v. 10).

The fact that God is the Lord of history implies that all that occurs serves His purpose, whether in one way or another. The fall of Samaria to the Assyrians in the eighth century B. C. was so completely under God's control that God could call Assyria the rod of His anger (Isaiah 10:5). And yet, after God had used

Assyria to fulfill His purpose. He humbled and destroyed it (Isaiah 10:12, 24–27). So totally are foreign nations and rulers in God's hand that he can call Cyrus, the Persian ruler through whose decree the dispersed Israelites will eventually return to their land, His shepherd and His anointed (Isaiah 44:28, 45:1).

What this adds up to is that all of history fulfills the sovereign purposes of God, both for nations and for individuals.

Anthony A. Heokema
The Bible and the Future
Eerdman's Publishing Company
(printed by permission)

Jesus Christ and History

The second coming of Christ will not be an event arising out of history; nor will it be the result of other historical events. It will be a free act of God, breaking into history in the person of the glorified Christ, to redeem history from the evils of the centuries and to transform it into the kingdom of God. It will be without real analogy. The incarnation was indeed an invasion into history from God's world, and so may seem partly analogous. But in the incarnation, the coming of God was veiled. Only the eye of faith could behold His glory (John 1:14); even His own friends thought Jesus was insane (Mark 3:21). The second coming of Christ will be a glorious in-breaking of the power of God, by which God will do for history and for mankind what neither history nor man can do for themselves.

Here is the fundamental meaning of the second coming of Christ for history. Man cannot redeem himself, nor can history produce the Kingdom of God. Perverted by sin, man has lost his way. Burdened by evil, history of itself is doomed. Speaking as a purely "objective" historian, Bultmann rightly describes the search for meaning in history as meaningless. Such familiar names as Auschwitz and Dachau speak of the snarl of irrational and demonic threads in the warp and woof of history, which men cannot weave into meaningful and purposeful pattern.

The gospel is the good news that God has abandoned neither man nor history. In the incarnation of Christ, God has invaded human history to defeat the forces of evil that man cannot conquer. In the second coming of Christ, God will again invade history to finish the redeeming work He has begun. Redemption from beginning to end is the work of God who transcends history. The return of Christ is the means by which redemption will be consummated. Even so come, Lord Jesus!

G. E. Ladd
Jesus Christ and History
Intervarsity Press, 1963
(printed by permission)

Implications for the Present Age

1. We live between the two "invasions": the _____ and the
   _____.

2. To use a World War II analogy, we live between _____-Day and
   _____ Day.
   - _____-Day – the success of the Normandy invasion made
     victory _____.
   - The consummation of the victory was not realized until _____
     Day, when the surrender occurred and fighting ended.
   - Christ's victory over sin and death were secured at the _____
     and _____. The final consummation of the victory will take
     place at the _____ _____.

3. During this "in between" time, the kingdom of _____ and the
   kingdom of _____ will _____. At the final judgment, the
   "wheat and tares" will be separated. Matthew 13:24–30, 36–43.

4. The focus of our time in history is _____.
   - Matthew ____:____ — The _____ _____ was mandated
     for all believers.
   - Matthew ____:____ — The _____ is to be preached throughout
     the whole _____, to all _____. Then shall the
     _____ come.
   - Acts 1:8 indicates an ever _____ preaching of the gospel.
   - 1 Peter 3:15 — We must be prepared to give a _____ for the
     hope within us, to offer the hope of the _____ to a
     _____ world.

5. The purpose of this course is not only to understand men's ideas and
   strengthen our _____ in God's truth but to _____
   us to spread the _____ to those around us.

   2 Corinthians 6:2 _____ is the day of _____.

18 THE WAY THINGS REALLY ARE

Scripture Search

Colossians 2:8 _____
_____

John 14:6 _____
_____

John 17:14–18 _____
_____

2 Corinthians 10:3–5 _____
_____

2 Chronicles 7:14 _____
_____

Colossians 1:9–14 _____
_____

2 Timothy 2:15 _____
_____

1 Chronicles 12:32 _____
_____

Psalm 11:3 _____
_____

Proverbs 22:28 _____

_____

Acts 1:8 _____

_____

Matthew 28:18–20 _____

_____

Revelation 5:12–14 _____

_____

Revelation 21:1–5 _____

_____

Psalm 118:6 _____

_____

Ezekiel 22:30 _____

_____

1 John 5:4 _____

_____

Psalm 9:8 _____

_____

Vocabulary Review

Review the definitions of the following terms as well as some identifying information for the personalities listed.

Introduction
worldview
atheism
pantheism
Christian theism
materialism
Humanist Manifestoes I and II
Prometheus Books
Karl Marx
Vladimir Lenin
Frederick Engels
Joseph Stalin
John Dewey
Paul Kurtz
Isaac Asimov
Carl Sagan
Julius Huxley
Eric Fromm
Shirley MacLaine

Theology
general revelation
special revelation
inspiration

Ethics
ethical relativism

Philosophy
anthropology
cosmology
epistemology
ethics
metaphysics
ontology

monism
assumption
presupposition
dualism
agnosticism
deism
dialectic
thesis
antithesis
synthesis
naturalism
mind precedes matter
matter precedes mind
faith precedes reason

Biology
spontaneous generation
punctuated equilibrium
natural selection
survival of the fittest
Charles Darwin

Psychology
self-actualization
behaviorism
B. F. Skinner
Ivan Pavlov
Abraham Maslow

Sociology
proletariat
bourgeoisie
collectivism
individualism
pluralism

Law
positive law
positivism
natural law

Politics
democracy-differs
according to worldview

Economics
capitalism (free enterprise)
socialism (collectivism)
communism
comparative advantage
Liberation Theology

History
nihilism
historical materialism
economic determinism
linear history
incarnation
Great Commission
Providence

Enrichment Activity: Letter from the Big U

Problem		Response
	Dear Dub,	

Greetings from the big "U"!
College life is really something.
I'm learning new ideas, meeting
new people, and enjoying being on
my own.

It seems people here view life from
a lot of different perspectives. I
guess that makes sense because of
their different backgrounds. I'm
trying to, you know, be more
accepting of different ideas. I'm
learning to be more open-minded.
After being here it seems like, well,
it's like the Bible is so narrow.
There seem to be other religious
ideas that really help people, too. I
guess it just boils down to what
works for you. I just don't feel
right pushing my faith on others.

My biology class is really interesting. I never knew there was so
much fossil evidence for evolution.
I mean, they talk about evolution
so matter-of-factly that it seems
stupid to question it. I wonder if
our science and Bible teachers at
our Christian school ever heard
this evidence for evolution.

Problem

Response

I met this other Christian student named Carl. He said maybe evolution was too complicated to explain in the Bible so God may have designed Genesis 1–11 as kind of an allegory, like a story to illustrate what happened rather than a description. Maybe evolution and the Bible aren't in conflict at all. I never really thought about it that way before. I guess you can't argue with the facts!

I met this interesting guy named Shakin. His name used to be George until he changed religions. He's a really patient, kind, calm guy. In all the pressure of his studies as a graduate student here, he still has real peace. It seems he believes that all life is one and that we find inner peace by meditating. He says his source of peace is within and that this is true for all men who are really enlightened. It's really something. I mean, he has no guilt or worry. It works for him! When he has to make a decision he meditates and then he says he just knows what to do! Must be nice!

Problem

My religion professor is a demanding teacher. Professor Rigidnoz believes that the Bible contains the Word of God but that parts of it are probably not really inspired. I guess that's reasonable. I mean, why would God inspire all those "begats" and those odd ceremonial laws in Leviticus? The prof says there is a lot of oral tradition and myths mixed in with the history which makes it hard to study. I'm glad we have scholars like Dr. Rigidnoz to get to the bottom of all that for the rest of us so that we'll know what to believe.

It seems other religions have myths about a big flood too, so maybe the Bible is not so unique after all. I wonder if it is really as reliable as we were taught to believe? I wonder how anyone could tell about a book that old? We don't even have the original

Oh, well, you can tell I'm really learning a lot here at the "U". Gotta sign off now and head for the big game! Will write more later . . .

Ed

Response

Enrichment Activity: Letter to the Editor

Problem

Response

Dear Editor:

I am appalled at the action of the fanatic religious right. Their opposition to the proposed homosexual rights ordinance is deplorable. You can't legislate morality. What business is it of theirs anyway. When two adults want to practice homosexual sex, that's a private decision. You people can't push your old fashioned morality on the rest of us.

If that isn't enough, these religious meddlers keep picketing our local abortion clinic. Give it up! Abortion is legal. Our society has determined that abortion is not immoral. Why bring unwanted children into this world? Doesn't a woman have a right to control her own body?

Let's keep religion in the churches where it belongs!

Sincerely,

O. Pen Minded

Enrichment Activity: Letter from College II

Problem

Response

Dear Sarah,

Greetings to my best friend back home. We are trying to get used to living in Campbellville but it's still rather lonely. Dad's new job seems to be working out OK and I've started classes at the Community College.

My humanities class is really interesting. My professor is like — wow — smart! he sees all these deeper meanings and stuff in all these books we have to read. He even assigned part of the Bible to read. He says he wants us to think for ourselves about life and get away from the old ideas we were taught at home. He really respects us adults and acts like he trusts us. That's really neat! It's so different from high school where our teachers checked up on us all the time.

We read this story the other day about a political prisoner having to lie to escape to get back to his family. Then he killed a guard and stole a bunch of stuff. Anyway, we had to figure out if what he did was wrong or not depending on how it all came out. What a mind boggler. I guess things are not always clearly right or wrong. Life is more complicated than I thought.

Problem

I met a girl at work who is so nice. We have become good friends. She is very considerate of others, and I think she mentioned going to church a while back. Wow, was I surprised to find out she's living with her boyfriend! When I seemed surprised she explained that her mom had been through two divorces, and she wasn't going to risk that. She wanted to be sure they could live together before she made a commitment. I never thought about it quite like that before. I don't want to judge her or anything. Actually, she's been nicer to me than some of my Christian friends.

The weirdest thing happened the other day. I was in the student center and I noticed two guys in the snack bar. They were real cute. I think one of them is in my English class. Anyway, it looked like they were holding hands under the table! Then they left and went by the bulletin board and put up a flyer for the next campus gay students' organization meeting. I couldn't believe it. Maybe gays aren't really the weirdos we thought. I don't guess they're hurting anyone so I guess it's live and let live on the college scene.

Gotta go now. Write soon!

Your friend,

Edna

Response

Enrichment Activity: Simulated News Article

New Law School President Addresses Faculty

In his inaugural address yesterday, U. R. Whiterock, newly appointed president of the State Law School, called for a forward orientation for the prestigious institution.

"We must embrace the responsibility to redefine the legal system for the needs of today by training the next generation of lawyers," he said. President Whiterock went on to encourage court rulings rejecting the privacy of citizens, citing Roe v. Wade as a commendable example.

"An earlier generation sought to appeal to the outmoded values of their forefathers for legal guidance. As man's thinking has progressed upward over the generations, he has departed from traditional religious law to a legal system that adapts to meet the needs of the day."

"We must spare no effort to protect the rights of the individual citizen, black or white, male or female, native or immigrant, heterosexual or homosexual, young or old. The morality of this generation will be determined in the courts. We must move ahead with the legal implementation of the admirable values of toleration, peace, and freedom for each citizen. Government must help the courts in establishing the rights of the citizens and resist limiting the freedom of the individual," Whiterock said.

President Whiterock will teach a seminar entitled "Positivism —The Practice of Law in a Post Blackstone America" in addition to his duties as president.

FOUR MODELS OF WESTERN RELIGIOUS THOUGHT

	Secular Humanism	Marxism/ Leninism	Cosmic Humanism	Biblical Christianity
THEOLOGY				
PHILOSOPHY				
ETHICS				
BIOLOGY				
PSYCHOLOGY				

FOUR MODELS OF WESTERN RELIGIOUS THOUGHT (con't)

	Secular Humanism	Marxism/ Leninism	Cosmic Humanism	Biblical Christianity
SOCIOLOGY				
LAW				
POLITICS				
ECONOMICS				
HISTORY				

FOUR MODELS OF WESTERN RELIGIOUS THOUGHT

	Secular Humanism	Marxism/ Leninism	Cosmic Humanism	Biblical Christianity
THEOLOGY				
PHILOSOPHY				
ETHICS				
BIOLOGY				
PSYCHOLOGY				

FOUR MODELS OF WESTERN RELIGIOUS THOUGHT (cont')

	Secular Humanism	Marxism/ Leninism	Cosmic Humanism	Biblical Christianity
SOCIOLOGY				
LAW				
POLITICS				
ECONOMICS				
HISTORY				

FOUR MODELS OF WESTERN RELIGIOUS THOUGHT

	Secular Humanism	Marxism/ Leninism	Cosmic Humanism	Biblical Christianity
THEOLOGY				
PHILOSOPHY				
ETHICS				
BIOLOGY				
PSYCHOLOGY				

FOUR MODELS OF WESTERN RELIGIOUS THOUGHT (con't)

	Secular Humanism	Marxism/Leninism	Cosmic Humanism	Biblical Christianity
SOCIOLOGY				
LAW				
POLITICS				
ECONOMICS				
HISTORY				

FOUR MODELS OF WESTERN RELIGIOUS THOUGHT

	Secular Humanism	Marxism/Leninism	Cosmic Humanism	Biblical Christianity
THEOLOGY				
PHILOSOPHY				
ETHICS				
BIOLOGY				
PSYCHOLOGY				

FOUR MODELS OF WESTERN RELIGIOUS THOUGHT *(con't)*

	Secular Humanism	Marxism/ Leninism	Cosmic Humanism	Biblical Christianity
SOCIOLOGY				
LAW				
POLITICS				
ECONOMICS				
HISTORY				

124